KENTLAND COOPER'S

SERIES I - A Mother's Love

Aya Emanuel

ISBN 978-1-957943-55-8 (paperback)
ISBN 978-1-957943-56-5 (hardcover)
ISBN 978-1-957943-57-2 (digital)

Rushmore Press LLC
1 800 460 9188
www.rushmorepress.com

Printed in the United States of America

INTRODUCTION

This book is written from memories.

Names have been changed to protect the true identity of living family members and friends.

This book is based on stories which I can recall and care to share. To make the book more interesting, it will also contain fiction such as character names (as mentioned above), and other information. Another way of protecting my family members and friends from being identified.

As the author, I thank you for taking the journey into my past and creative mind. I hope this book brings you joy, laughter and knowledge.

Welcome and Enjoy as you venture into...

I was born and raised by my mother Pauline Ebo Cooper and John Reed Cooper. My father was in my life until the age of 13 and my mother until the age of 28.

Unfortunately, I lost both of my parents to Cancer. My father less than 1 month after my 13th birthday.

At the age of 28, one year after my last baby was born, I then lost my mother.

The Big "C" is what we all called it. Cancer, my enemy and such an ugly disease which some of the body's cells grow uncontrollably and spread to other parts of the body. I call it life's enemy, snooping around to steal our most precious love ones with little to no notice at all.

Oh, how sweet my memories are to have had them both as my parents.

Chapter 1

THE BEGINNING

I was told by my elder sisters, aunts, and others in my family that my mother was a beautiful slim, dark skinned woman shaped like a Coca-Cola bottle. In other words, curvy.

By the time I was born in March 1964. My mother was a heavyset dark skin woman, with a belly that looked as if she was expecting another child. Still, she was very beautiful. Although, you could see the maturity of age in her face, that had now become a part of her beauty.

Her eyes always seem to have a glorious happiness to them. However, if you looked deeply, you could see the story of all that she had been through behind them.

She had such an enlightening smile, that when you looked upon her, you couldn't help but smile yourself. Her spirit was magnificent, truly of an angel. Kind and gentle.

A truly amazing women, she was blessed. I am sure she is still amazing in the afterlife as well. As for me, I simply adored my mother. Her smile, her laughter and her snuggling hugs.

When my mother hugged you, it gave you a sense of comfort and you felt the love. It was almost like magic. Meaning, if anything was on your mind causing you discomfort, her hugs would make you feel as though everything would be alright.

Her hugs always gave me strength, power, and a since of self-belief, encouragement and motivation to keep moving forward. She didn't have to say one word. Just her hug alone was enough to make me feel like a load was lifted off of me whenever I had any worries at all.

It was if, she would give you some of her positive energy and joy, and all of your worries vanished like magic.

It felt like she would simply take whatever worries, you may be going through off of you and onto her. If one could have looked deep into her soul, you probably would see many peoples' heavy weighted stories which she freed them of.

Once you came out of her hugs, you felt as though you had renewed strength, confidence and pride, and she would always remind you of who you were and who really held the power of all men and women.

My mother made you remember that there is nothing too large or too small for the creator above. Her love was outstanding.

She had 7 children and truly loved each and every one of us unconditionally. She made sure we all felt her love and that we all felt special. She never once favored one over the other.

Although at times, one did require more attention than the other. Meaning, we all had different challenges which required her to treat each of us according to our own needs in order for her to help us through life. We were her world and she was ours.

Love; 1ˢᵗ Corinthians 13:13 New International Version; "And now these three remain; Faith, Hope and Love. But the greatest of these is Love".

Love is truly powerful, and my mother's LOVE was indeed just that!

Growing up as a Cooper child, we didn't have much. We didn't have a lot of money, but we had a lot of love for one another. We had both our parents love, family love and friends. Our foundation of love and family was strong, and if you were fortunate enough to have a Cooper as your friend, truly pulled into that Cooper family circle, it was loyalty and genuine true friendship until the end. Family is forever.

It's one thing I used to love to hear from my mother that made a great impact on me as a child and as an adult. One thing out of many that stayed with me the most, was when and how she would say that she was so proud of me. Those words gave me encouragement and strength to continue to do what I felt was the right thing. Those words filled my heart up and still does until this day. It continues to bring a smile to my face and tears to my eyes when I am told that from someone whom I know really means it. The words "I'm proud of you" (if truthfully meant), touches ones' heart with a feeling. I can't describe the feeling, but it feels so good when those words come dancing into your ears and heart. Say it loud or gentle, as small as a whisper, or even a special look without saying a word. It all gives joy. At least it feels that way to me, I've always been someone who tried to make others happy. Throughout my life, I've strived to be like my mother in that way. I guess that's where I get it from.

I sometimes close my eyes and just enjoy my memories.

My dad lost his fight with Lung Cancer and my mom to Pancreatic Cancer.

That Cancer moved so fast that it barely allowed us to say our goodbyes.

August 28th, she caught three buses to a doctor's appointment to see about her stomach, which had been bothering her for a while. Unfortunately, September the 12th she was gone. Less than one (1) month.

For many years, I was highly upset at the doctors because I felt like, how could she be healthy enough to catch three (3) buses to the doctors, drink that nasty stuff they gave her to drink and later that evening have to be rush back to the hospital in an Ambulance. Then the same night, be admitted into the hospital to never come home again.

It was just unreal to me. All I kept asking myself was what happen and what was in that stuff she drank. I had so many questions.

When the doctors spoke to us as a family to tell us there was no more they could do for her, I asked the question "what happen, how could she have been fine one day and then... (as the tears rolled down my face)", the doctor said, "it's a possibility that she had it for a while." He also said that most cancers come from the foods we eat and the way we cook our foods. One thing I will never forget he said was, "one (1) or two (2) of you will most likely go the same way. He said this was due to studies that have proven that families copy the same styles of their history. In other words, it was traditions that proved this theory. This means, we learn to cook like our parents, and we do as we are taught by our parents. So, history is bound to repeat itself.

As my mother was journeying into the afterlife. My mother said to us lying in that hospital bed "I want you all to stop all that drinking". See my mother use to drink with my dad and she continued to drink even after my dad passed when I was 13 years old. However, she had stopped drinking a long time ago before she got sick and passed away.

She had turned her life back around living right and walking in the right direction with the Lord again. She was going back to church on a regular basis and had stopped drinking.

She had stopped all those drinking buddies from coming over to the house and all the house parties had stopped as well. I mean when my mother put her foot down, she really put it down and shut it all off with a firm hand. Enough was enough and all of this was way before she got sick. Our house was spotless, it was clean again and quite. No more liquor bottles anywhere.

You would not believe it was the same house that use to be jumping with parties all the time.

To this day, I kept a lock of her hair from the front of her head. She had a small portion of her hair which hung down in her face. It was a beautiful black and gray wavy peace of hair. I cut a small piece of it off after she passed away. I remember leaning over her body, hugging her, crying and kissing her face. Enough tears falling from my eyes that could have flooded that entire hospital building.

That same piece of hair is still in her old bible, which I kept. From time to time, I take it out of the sandwich bag, which I have folded up in her obituary and placed inside her bible and just feel and smell it. Just remembering.

Although it's been over 27 years, I still smell her hair scent when I pull it out. Perhaps it's me just imagining it, but nevertheless, it feels so good to feel and smell her.

I can still hear her voice so clearly calling me from downstairs, yelling up stair's telling me to wake up and get ready for school.

Yelling up stair's telling my brother Samuel to "get out of that bathroom and go wake up your sister, so she can get in there and not miss that school bus"! The school bus to Charles Carroll Jr. High School in New Carrollton, MD.

I love and miss my mother so very much, and I am so very thankful I had a mom like her. I have nothing but wonderful memories of her.

To God be the Glory for allowing her to be my mom.

I remember my mother sharing with me, she had ten (10) pregnancies but only seven (7) survived.

She had four (4) girls and three (3) boys. All three of my brothers were named from the Bible;

David, Samuel and Jeremiah. The girls were named Brenda, Monica, Cassandra, and me.

The first child she gave birth to was a girl, which she and my dad named Brenda.

I was told my father wanted and was hoping their first child would be a boy, just as any first-time father would hope for.

According to what my mother told me, my dad was going to call the boy Bobby, but since it was a girl, they named her Brenda.

My oldest sister is 16 ½ years older than me. She is now in her early 70's and looks fabulous. Brenda is a caramel complexion woman, who has beautiful brown eyes and when she smiles it's sweet and genuine.

She was born in the month of May. Her zodiac sign is Gemini and she has always said; her sign is "twins" and she never knows what the other twin will do.

Chapter 2

MESSAGE RECEIVED

Well, let me just share a memory with you that I certainly remember what her other "twin side" did.

This was the time after my father had passed away and one of my brother's tried to flex his muscles at my mother.

My mother was on the phone talking to my big sister Brenda who didn't live far from us. As a matter of fact, she lived up the street from our house in the Landover area of Palmer Park Md.

The house faced the Landover Rd side of Palmer Park. So, it was very easy for Brenda to just jump into her car and come directly down the street to our house. Heck, we walked up and down Landover Rd several times going back and forth to my sister's house.

Apparently, my mother had been telling her over the phone about how my brother was being disrespectful to her. Either my mother told her, or Brenda overheard some of the conversation through the phone.

All of a sudden, before my mother knew it, my sister was no longer on the phone. She was coming through the front door looking for my big brother.

My big brother started running through the house and went running up the steps trying to get away from her.

Brenda took out her small handgun, shot one time up the stairs behind him, and luckily for him she missed.

Now I never knew if she intentionally missed, and just shot to scare him, but she missed. My big brother certainly got the message and so did the rest of the family.

What message; I guess the message was that our dad may be gone, but Big Sis is not. No one living in that house, better not ever try mother again.

Message was well received.

Later through the years as we grew up, some of my siblings tried my mother again, a few more times. However, since big sis was like our dad, quick to shoot, I believe those other times my mother may have decided not to share it with her right-away.

My mother and Brenda were indeed the best of friends. So, believe me when I say, I am sure she told her, just not until it was long over with.

You see, as the story goes and what was shared with me about my oldest sister Brenda, when she was younger she was not to be played with, she had that Cooper fire in her blood as well... know doubt. They said she too had a sexy out of this world shape, like my mother use to have.

Almost all the guys in her school was crazy about that Cooper girl. She had beautiful long thick black hair, was a very talented majorette dancer for her High School in Washington, DC and could twirl that baton like no other.

They said, that little short Cooper girl would set you straight in the minute. A furious Lion in a cat's body.

She is now in her early 70's and you would look at her and not believe she is even in her late 50's.

As of today, she now has a head full of beautiful silver/gray hair.

However, she pretty much like to keep her hair in locks or braids, sometimes with color, sometimes without.

She is still slim and sexy and even at the age of 70 plus, she still looks great.

One thing is, she works out, eats right and enjoys life. She loves and I mean loves children and animals.

Brenda has been married for over 50 plus years to her school sweetheart, and she and my brother-in-law (one of the best brother-in-law's, one could ever ask for), is still very much happily in love and the very best of friends just as the first day they met.

I love Brenda. I thank her and my brother-in-law for the wonderful memories they gave me as a child and what they continue to do for me throughout my adult life.

They are wonderful to my children, my grandchildren and even my dog loves them.

To me, the two of them helped to keep our family infrastructure strong when our dad was living and long after he passed away. It's as if the two of them became the father figure of support for our mother after our dad passed away.

I thank both of them for helping my mother with her five (5) children.

Chapter 3

DOLL BABY

The second child my parents had, was also another girl and they named her Monica, after my mother's mother (Monica Ebo, born in the late 1890's).

My two older sisters (unlike the rest of us, were not born in the Washington DC area), they were both born in Asheville, North Carolina and then raised in NE Washington, DC.

Brenda and Monica didn't live in our home in Kentland. They were both much older than the rest of us who did. Since they were both grown and married, they had their own homes by the time we moved to Kentland.

Although, it's not a lot that will be mentioned about them in this book, they will be mentioned.

My sister Monica was nicked name by my father who called her "Baby Doll, Doll Baby". So, the rest of family and friends just called her Doll. All except my father and my cousin, who we will call Bernard (for the sake of privacy).

Now that I think of it, I also remember my sister Doll having another boyfriend (let's call him Bright light) who sometimes called her Doll Baby and Baby Doll also.

Doll and my cousin Bernard were around the same age and they were extremely close. The best of friends.

Doll was a sexy, very hippy short women who truly loved to dress and could dress her behind off. Heck she was wearing red bottom shoes before I even knew what they were.

Chapter 4

A COUSIN'S LOVE

Bernard was from Winston Salem West Virginia and he was a big country guy.

He was over 6ft tall, and a very, strongly built. A handsome country man. Sort of a lumberjack looking guy.

The way it looked to me, was all women loved him. However, the only women he seemed to be interested in, was anything other than black women.

The majority of the time his preference was Caucasian women. As long as they were not black, they had a chance with him.

I always wondered if something happened to him in his past with black females. You know, perhaps in the past, a black woman broke his heart and maybe he simply never recovered.

I don't know but that was something to wonder about for sure.

Nevertheless, that didn't bother me one bit. Love is love and it doesn't matter what color you are as long as you love that person, and treat each other with respect, kindness and love. It's all good. At least that is how I feel about it.

Bernard, from time to time, actually did date mulattoes. It seemed that was as close to black as he would get. I do recall him having one mulatto girl that I knew very well, and she was cool people (at least I thought so).

To me she was more so a young girl than a woman because she was younger than I was, and I was extremely younger than Bernard.

However, she was of age when she and my cousin started dating so it was perfectly legal, even though she was much, much younger than him and such a tiny girl. No doubt she could have past as his daughter. Just their size alone would make you take a double look if you saw them together.

I am 5'2 and I believe not only was she younger than me, but she was much shorter than me as well.

Her name was Jamie and I must say, she was certainly a pretty girl, a beautiful girl actually. Just to give you an image… picture a young pretty Mariah Carey, that's about how she looked. I think she once told me her mom was German and her dad was mixed with black. However, for some reason she felt she was a true African American. "Power to the people" kind of person. Peace and Soul type of sister.

And I had absolutely no problem with that at all.

As I said, it didn't bother me one bit. I try not to judge others. My mother taught us better than that.

Chapter 5

JUDGMENT OF OTHERS

*U*nfortunately, when I got older, I learn that there are people out there that will look at you and although they know nothing about you, they will judge you according to various things and not even take the time to get to know you.

Just by looking at you, they have already made their decision about you because of the color of your skin, the shape of your noise, the family you are a part of or became a part of perhaps through Forster Care, the neighborhood you live in and the people you associate yourself with.

Another thing I learned is that sometimes we are harder on ourselves than we should be. Meaning, we judge ourselves unfairly and at times, never allowing ourselves the opportunity to grow and enjoy things that life presents to us. Comparing ourselves with others. Wishing we had what someone else may have. Like straighter or longer hair, being taller or even our weight.

Fear played a big part in my life. I loved to write songs and sing but I was always afraid of what people would think of me. So, I decided not to move forward with going after my dream.

Life is so sweet, and the creator has blessed us all with a talent. Most of us, including myself at one time, are afraid to step out and go get what is truly ours. We are so concerned about being judged by others that we allow the fear to step in and keep us from reaching for the stars.

I used to always say "Reach for the moon and even if you miss, you will be among the stars". I read that somewhere when I was younger. Although I always remembered it and repeated it to others quite often, even I though sometimes I never applied it to my own life.

Our gifts are ours and we should use them. Step out on faith and believe in the love and power of our creator and allow all that belief to take off like a rocket.

Faith;

Luke 17:6;

"And the Lord answered, "If you have faith the size of a mustard seed, you can say to this mulberry tree, 'Be uprooted and planted in the sea, 'and it will obey you."

"faith the size of a mustard seed" is **ALL** we need, and the almighty creator will do the rest.

I've always said; Life is what we make it and a lot of us fear making it what we desire it to be for us.

This includes me. It took a lot out of me to finish this book which I started over 12 years ago, and still I had to make it a series because there is so much more to share. However, I decided instead of continuing the book in its entirety, I will make it a series to allow me to accomplish what seems to have been almost a lifetime dream. Pray on it, let go and let God.

Over the past couple of years, I have been visualizing receiving a check an extensive large amount of funds, a vision. I believe in the saying, "see it, believe it, and speak it into existence". You know the saying, "If you can believe it, you can achieve it".

Well, I am writing this book from memories and I also write song lyrics. I've been writing them for years. I never did anything with either one besides enjoy them myself with family and friends. So, this time, I am going to try something different. Sharing it with the world.

Chapter 6

JUDGMENT OF OTHERS (CONT.)

*B*ack to the story;

As I was saying;

People have already made their decision about you just by looking at you. Unfortunately, before they even try to get to know you, they've made up their minds about you. That's just something we can never escape.

If your father was a drunk, naturally they believed you were one or at least will become one because as the old saying goes…"the apple doesn't fall far from the tree".

Well, let me just tell you, that is not always true either. Sometimes coming from, as some would call "a dysfunctional background", makes you work harder to ensure your future and your children's future, (including grand and great grandchildren) never ever have to experience what you had to experience as a child.

Unfortunately, as a child, the majority of the time you have no power to change anything. The fact that you were a child and had no choice in the decisions made for you, fortunately, made a great difference in your life. However, once you became grown enough to make a decision for your own life, you did. With the hopes that you made the right decisions. I know I did and not only for me, but I dreamt all the time to try to make it as a songwriter and singer to better my family life. I know my brother's dream was to make it as a boxer to better our family's life. We all wanted a much better life, no doubt. I can recall each of us doing something trying to follow a path which we believed could have made our dreams come true. Unfortunately, sometimes life throws you a curveball causing you to lose your focus or you get sidetracked.

People can be so quick to judge others. It hurts to know that some never stepped out of their comfort zone and just for a second, try to think of what another individual might be going through.

There are people in the world today, living in the streets, prostituting, in jails, and some suffer from mental illnesses. But more simply enough, because it's a reaction that generated from an action which happened while they were a child, their lives took a turn for the worst. They did not choose to live that way.

Some are not strong enough to have survived what sometimes being a child in certain situations can bring on.

A dysfunctional family or a divorce (which I learned in my adult life), can cause tremendous pain to an individual and make a difference in the outcome of your life. One can either think positive and get through it or take the negative approach and believe "since they say I am nothing, then I am nothing" which is the easy way out and oh so sad.

You also have some people who compare themselves to the misfortunate ones to gain strength from their misfortune. Meaning, believing they are better than other people simply because they were fortunate enough not to have to live in a lifestyle such as other misfortunate ones.

People who believe they are better because they had both a mom and dad, when someone else only had one parent. Perhaps their parent or parents had good paying jobs, fancy cars, didn't drink, smoke or party.

Some people believe, simply because their skin is lighter, or they live in a better neighborhood up the street, down the street or even around the corner from the misfortunate ones, or in a whole different community, they have the right to look down on those who are less fortunate.

Unfortunately, there is also a flipside where the individual who has all of what I mentioned above (great homes, parents doing well and light complexion, fancy cars, etc.), also go through the discomfort of being identified as thinking that they are better when they truly do not.

All they want is not to be judge according to the color of their skin or any other things. They simply hurt inside for being considered different and therefore, they too suffer from being falsely judged by others. The judgement cycle seems like it never ends.

I remember the first time I first realized that I was actually on the side of the skin tone which some consider "to dark", the unacceptable side…OMG!! How very painful it was for me.

See my mother never judged anyone for their skin color. Our family was of a mixture, a Varity of colors. Some of us are bright-light damn near white and others are dark as the tar in the streets. But we are all family.

We have white, Indian and African in our blood and more. My mother informed us all that we need not be surprised if a child of ours or our grandchildren came out dark with blue eyes because it is a possibility.

My mother was so beautiful inside and out that we were not raised to see color at all.

But as I grew up into this big beautiful world, I noticed that sometimes ugly shows up more often than I cared to see.

I truly had my experience with it and found out that yes, some people in this world can't get passed the differences of others, like the color of your skin, the way you wear your hair, the size of your noise, and even the shape of your eyes.

I heard someone say in the old days regarding colored slaves, that the darkies worked in the field while the lighter ones worked in the house because most of the time, the light skin ones were considered the master's child.

What some people simply don't get is that both dark skin and light skin people were still slaves. We were all considered color children.

We were separated according to our skin by the master and unfortunately, it made some start to feel they indeed were better than others.

Well, I found out after being bused to Jr high school that it's true, people truly judged you according to your skin color.

Yes, it took me to leave elementary school and the Kentland community to see that there is sometimes ugliness in this big beautiful world. Perhaps in elementary school, I was too young to notice the difference.

Perhaps it was at that school as well, but it didn't stand out to me at all. Again, maybe I was just too young to have noticed it. Whatever the case, I didn't feel it until high school. Besides, when you're a child, you are of pure innocence.

I remember being in the work release program in high school and I went on an interview. Mr. Ugly stood up and said to me, in so many words, "don't even try it darkie. At least that is how I felt.

Yes, the ugliness of racism showed up and reared its ugly head. If you were light skin with good hair and a pointy noise, you were alright and most of the time accepted. If you were darker than a paper bag, well let's just say you had to work much harder than the others in everything you did.

I remember the school counselor sent me and another girl on a job interview. The girl was light-skinned and pretty, with pretty hair.

Although we attended the same high school, we had never met before, we had passed each other in the hall in school and said hello from time to time.

She was a very nice girl and as we sat waiting on the ride to the interview, I really enjoyed chatting with her.

These were jobs where a student would go to school for a ½ day, and then leave and go to work. I believe it was called The Work Study Program.

Well we were both dropped off at the building and as we were sitting outside in the hallway of an office within the building, this skinny white lady came out of the door, took one look at the both of us and said, "we only have a need for one of you so we are just going to select you". Then she pointed to the pretty light skin girl. The women walked over to us both and looked directly at me in my eyes and said, "we don't need you. We will notify your school if we need another person". At that point, she asked the girl to follow her and they went down the hall into another room.

Believe it or not, even the girl looked like she knew that wasn't right. I mean she was happy she was selected but she also looked surprised and hurt for me. It was just the way the lady looked at me. The tone of her voice wasn't very pleasant either.

As I waited for the ride to come back to pick me up, I actually cried. I guess I was feeling a little self-pity for myself. All I could see was how proud my mother would have been if I had gotten the job and how much I could have helped her with our family.

When I got home and told my mother what had happened, she just held me. She said, "it's ok baby". She told me that God had something better for me. Once again, I cried in her arms and as always came out rejuvenated.

However, I did learn on that painful day that this world can truly be ugly at times.

Chapter 7

COMMUNITY TOGETHERNESS

I guess in elementary school, I didn't feel the ugliness. In Landover, MD we were all like Family. I mean at least I felt like we were all family. It just seemed like the people from our area, the Kentland area, was family. Even though we were all of different races, had different shades of skin, and were of different ethnic backgrounds. I mean, we were all from the same area, so it was all good. No one thought they were better than anyone.

It was always so much fun growing up in Kentland with what seemed to be family throughout almost the entire Landover, Md area.

Areas such as;

Kentland, Capitol Hill East, Dodge Park (where Martin Lawrence use to live), Kent-Village, Columbia Park, Strafford Woods, Palmer Park (where Sugar Ray Leonard the famous boxer use to live), Belhaven and Village Green were all sort of like family as well.

Those were the communities near Kentland that were in walking distance.

The whites who lived in those communities, had no problem with the blacks and the blacks had no problems with them. Though as time went on, most of the white and Indian families started moving out of the communities.

Everyone was like family and everyone's parents could put your behind in check if you were caught doing something wrong.

Back then, kids had more respect and cared if any adult saw them doing something wrong.

Black guys dated white girls and white guy's dated black girls and vice versa. That was never a problem in our neighborhood at all.

No one had a problem with it. At least, that's how I saw it back in the day. I was young so perhaps I didn't know any better.

My mother never explained to me that there was a difference. I am sure she didn't want to put that negativity of the world in my head. I was indeed a momma's girl so in the beginning, most of the time, I was up under my mother most of the time.

As for me and my children, I wanted to try to help my children get ready for this world, so I did share it with them when they got older.

It wasn't to plant negativity in their minds, but to make them aware of what's out there.

If you are not ready, this world will try hard to eat you up and spit you out with no remorse feelings about it at all. Simply because to them, you are different.

I wanted my children to know that no matter what, always remember, men do not hold the power.

Everything comes from the creator above.

I also ensured they knew, no matter what, I will always love them, no matter who they choose to love or what decisions they make in their life. I showed them and made sure that they knew that just because I may disagree with them, doesn't mean I've stopped loving them and I wanted them to always know that.

I did my best and I continue to do my best to show them my unconditional love. I am so thankful to the Lord for my children.

I have instilled in them, reminded them and guided them always to remember who holds all power and they are greatly knowledgeable of the King our Lord and Savor who is in control of all.

I am very proud of all of my children and their successes in life.

Chapter 8

CHILDREN ARE AWESOME

All three of my children are awesome!

I must pat my mother, myself, my ex-husband, my current husband and both sides of our family on the back for the way we all raised them up and supported them. My children are successful, truly outstanding, amazing, wonderful, loving respectful God-fearing children.

My sons remember my mother well, but my daughter was only one years old when we lost my mother. So, she didn't get to have an opportunity to get to know her. However, she has heard so many wonderful things about her that she feels she knows her just as well as her two brothers.

Thank you, Heavenly father "King Jesus" for the blessings.

Chapter 9

A COUSIN'S LOVE (CONT.)

My cousin Bernard's girlfriend Jamie must have been 15 years or more younger than him. Not to mention, she was 5-foot-tall, short slim girl and he was 6ft tall and a thick country man.

They ended up getting married and having children. I believe they live in the Caribbean's now.

After my mom passed away, we didn't see much of my cousin anymore. However, my oldest sister Brenda and my brother-in-law kept in touch with him from time to time.

I remember speaking to him once on the phone when he was in town and he stopped by my sister's house to see them. My sister called me, and I talked with him. It was a brief conversation, but it was still nice to know he was still alive and doing well.

Bernard, by size, was a man that actually could have been a football player, if they were picking men for their size and strength.

He was extremely smart and talented. He could play the heck out of a Piano. Just to give you an image of him, he could have been a linebacker on the defensive side. That's how strong and big he was.

If he were born into slavery, no doubt the master's would have look at him as one of the men they matched up to make "strong bucks", as the old-time slavery movies say.

The 1975 movie Mandingo crosses my mind when I think of my cousin.

Bernard was well liked by a lot of people and very much loved by family and friends.

He has such a big heart and he is such a kindhearted man. I remember a time when a house down the street caught on fire and it was taking the fire trucks way too long to arrive. What makes it so bad, the Kentland Fire Station was directly up the street.

Bernard ran into that burning house to save people and he did just that!

Unfortunately, he didn't know a baby was still asleep in another room. Once he got the lady out of the house and resuscitated her, the lady woke up screaming "my baby!!"

He tried to go back into the house, but the flames were just too large and unfortunately nor him or the firemen (when they finally arrived), could save the baby. That just broke his heart. When he thought he got everyone out before the fire trucks came and then he found out a baby was still in there. He cried so hard. It was so heartbreaking.

That wasn't the first time in my life that I saw him cry and it certainly wasn't the last. There was the time when we lost my dad. We knew he was passing, so there was time to prepare. However, the last time I saw him cry (which was truly devastating to him), was when we lost my mother. That was just as hurtful because of how sudden death came and stole her from us.

I love my cousin. He truly is a good man. He has to have a gold star for his bravery on the books in heaven for just that one act alone.

Although my cousin was well like, there was also some others that were scared of him and saw him as "crazy cousin Bernard". Some things some people would say about him, I could and will never allow myself to believe.

However, when he was drinking, he wasn't a man you wanted to play with. Especially if he wasn't in his right frame of mine. Other than that, to me he was always fun to be around.

I recall overhearing a story that one day after a few drinks he began driving home or somewhere (not quite sure where he was going). Apparently, he noticed a car going the same way that he was going and making the same turns he was making. So (in Bernard's drunk mind), the car was following him and when they stopped at a red light, Bernard got out of his car, walk to the car behind him and snatch the man clean out of the car window and beat that man bad, because he thought the man was following him.

Because the man made every turn my cousin made, my cousin said; "if he makes one more damn turn like I make...", and sure enough, the man did just that.

To this day, I don't believe that man knew who my cousin even was. Probably, never saw him a day in his life. He just happened to be going the same way that my cousin was going.

Unfortunately, in my cousin's mind, he felt like he was being followed by this man, especially since he was making all the same turns my cousin was making. So, when they both came to the stop light, my cousin approached the man and just went off on him and started beating the man up.

Now, I didn't witness that particular fight, but I remember my mother being told that my cousin was in jail again for drunk driving and beating up a man at a stop light.

There was another time that I actually did witness a fight for myself, between Bernard and Mr. G (a very nice man who was also about 6ft tall but very slim). Bernard started the "so called" fight.

Chapter 10

THE "SO CALLED FIGHT"

r. G (deceased now) was a good man as well. He was always happy and smiling every time I saw him.

Always positive and gave nothing but the best advice. A truly good man. I never heard Mr. G say or speak anything negative about anyone.

Mr. G would also call me "Peachy Pie" most of the time whenever he saw me.

A very nice man indeed, and good friend to my family and one of my daddy's closest neighborhood friends.

Mr. G also lived in Kentland. On the same street but down the hill from us, next door to my best friend.

Here is what I remember about this "so called" fight.

My cousin and Mr. G were also the best of friends. However, one day, they started "so called fighting". I call it "so called fighting" because Mr. G would not fight my cousin back at all.

I guess because he knew my cousin was drunk, it could be the reason why he decided to just keep away from him by running around the car.

Now, that I think about it, I guess it was best because although they were both 6ft tall, there is no way Mr. G would have been able to beat my cousin because he was just too strong, and I believe younger than Mr. G as well.

Plus, every last Cooper or family member with Cooper blood could fight like heck. My father served in WWII and could fight extremely well, so he taught all his sons how to fight.

All of my brothers were boxers. Not professionally, but they all grow up in the Sugar Ray Leonard Gym, two of them, even before it was called the Ray Leonard Gym.

Unfortunately, none of them actually made it as a professional boxer.

We did have one that was extremely close to becoming a professional. My big brother Samuel (name changed to protect his family). Although I never witnessed it, he told me that he was a sparring partner once, with a famous boxer from the Palmer Park area before.

One thing I do know for sure is that all of my brothers were a member of the Palmer Park Gym and my brother Samuel was trained by two of the best boxing trainers in my opinion.

At least this is what I recall and was informed of. I remember one of the trainers as a very nice slim dark skin man, and the other, as a very nice, sort of heavyset light skin man. He was well known as a famous trainer. I always thought of George Duke whenever I saw him, which was only a few times in person.

When you added liquor and the Cooper crazy bloodline on top of those tough fighting boxing skills, you've created a monster.

Chapter 11

THE "SO CALLED" FIGHT (CONT.)

Ok, so Bernard and Mr. G were both sitting outside the yard drinking on the corner standing next to a car talking, laughing, singing and having fun.

People including myself, was outside playing in the yard or around the yard. When out of nowhere, Bernard surprised Mr. G with a sucker punch or maybe push.

Now, I'm not really sure which one it was because all I saw was Mr. G fall on the ground and I heard him shot, "Bernard what's wrong with you man!!?".

I think that's probably what made Mr. G realize (as he was getting up off the ground), that something had changed and went terribly wrong without him knowing. He also had to feel that perhaps Bernard had enough to drink.

In the beginning, they were having a wonderful time. The drinks were in the car which they were standing near. It was obviously in that brown paper bag that I kept seeing them take in and out of the car.

Then all of a sudden, out of nowhere, the next thing I remember is Mr. G getting up off the ground saying, "Bernard what's wrong with you man??!! What you hit me for man??!! I didn't say nothing to you!!".

Mr. G was running around the car and my cousin was chasing him trying to catch him. He caught up to him one more time and knocked him down again. Mr. G rolled over and got up quickly and started running around the car again.

Now my cousin was a big man and I don't think he was trying to hurt Mr. G because he was more like pushing him down, not punching him, and Bernard could fight, he could fight well. So, I am not sure what that was all about.

However, someone went running into the house and told mother. She came outside and started yelling for them to stop. "I said stop it Bernard!! Stop it right now!" And believe it or not, it was over.

Yes, my mother came outside and when she spoke, that was it. Bernard was done chasing Mr. G and Mr. G was done running.

Bernard said, "well he shouldn't have said what he said". Mr. G was still screaming "Said what! what did I say!?"

Bernard said, "you know what the hell you said".

Back then I felt bad and pretty sad for Mr. G., and mad at my cousin for fighting him. Everyone else was laughing like crazy because it was like a comedy act. Two drunks carrying on.

After my mother had stopped the "so-called" fight and things had calmed down, they both went in the house with my mother.

At the dining room table, my mother help clean up Mr. G, getting all the dirt off of him and cleaning the little scrapes from when he fell down.

My cousin, was also sitting at the dining room table but at the other end of it, looking zoned out and stupidly mumbling, "well, he shouldn't had said it".

My mom, of course, got on them both for acting like children. Telling them that they were friends and grown men out there acting like children and that all the children were watching them behave like pure fools.

She told them that they needed to put that liquor down if they didn't know how to act.

She fed them some food and of course, it was all over. It was like, they were little boys who just got in trouble by their mom.

A little after that, they were friends again. Just like nothing had ever happened. Talking and laughing and everything.

After a short while, Mr. G walked down the street to his home and my cousin went outside on the side porch sofa and went to sleep. To this day, I never found out what the so called, fight was about. I don't think Mr. G did either.

Cousin Bernard was really cool. He loved my parents dearly and especially my mother. Although my mother wasn't his blood (because he was from my father side), it didn't make a difference to him, my mother was just so wonderful, and everyone loved her.

The power of her love was just amazing.

My cousin always called me Peachy Pie. Actually, I think he was the one who started calling me that first. My best friend still calls me that almost every time she gets tipsy.

Memories of my cousin, other than the "so called fight" with Mr. G, are all good ones, with one exceptional memory....

Chapter 12

STINKY FEET

I will never forget Bernard's, stinky feet.

My goodness, the memory of how bad his feet stunk or maybe it was his shoe boots because when he stayed the night and took off his shoe's, you could smell his feet from miles away.

You could tell he was in the house or on the side porch just as you walked through the front gate. You didn't even have to be at the front door yet, those dogs (his feet) were barking!

Just approaching the fence walking to and through the gate, you knew from that smell Country Cousin Bernard was in town.

I always wondered how he got so many women with feet smelling that bad once he took his shoes off.

Although, we couldn't stand the smell of his feet or shoe boots, we loved having him over. Other than his feet smelling, he was a clean man.

It was just that his feet or his shoes had an outstanding, noise burning, unbearable odor. That's why most of the time when he stayed, he slept outside on the side porch or in the basement. The few times he would fall asleep on the sofa in the living room, OMG! the entire house would light up.

Even when you tried to act like you didn't smell it, as if all was well, your face would show the look of "Got Damn!" Your face would show it every time. If you tried to smile, your eyes would squint up as you forced a smile on your face.

Your face would simply frown up because of the smell. I truly think it was a health condition he had with his feet.

My sweet mother would always say "alright now, go upstairs and wash up and wash your feet". She would put his shoes outside on the back porch or side porch and would always try to get the smell out the house. She was never nasty to him at all. As I said, we always loved having him around. It was just his feet.

Bernard was, most of the time, a lot of fun to have around He always gave us an extra sense of protection. At least, that's how I felt whenever he was around. He was very protective when he came to visit our family.

Chapter 13

DOLL BABY

lthough deceased now, Doll was the second oldest sister. A beautiful, dark skinned women that favored my father's Indian side.

Although my dad was fair skinned, my uncle Bill was a dark-skinned man with wavy jet-black hair and Doll was the spitting image of him. I was once told my uncle look just like his father (my granddad) except my uncle was shorter. Therefore, I suppose she got her looks from my grandfather.

She had dark black wavy hair (that good hair is what people call it). All she had to do was take a wet brush and poof, it was in a slick black sexy ponytail, bouncing with every step she took.

Doll was two years younger than Brenda and she had my mother's hips. She had a shape with hips that would make any man turn his head.

She was indeed a sexy woman who loved to dress, and she wore nothing but expensive clothes and shoes.

Every apartment she had, was laid out with unique furniture items, artifacts and other stuff. Stuff that you would see in furniture stores and think to yourself, "I wonder who would buy something like that". Well, Doll would have, and it would look fabulous! She could have been in movies.

She was a dark black beautiful baby doll indeed. She worked as a Casework for Prince Georges County and was 100% confident of herself and her success. She didn't need anyone to tell her that she was sexy and beautiful. Her walk spoke just that, confidence in every step.

All of this was of course long before the drugs and alcohol got a hold of her and tore her down to skin and bones, living the rest of her days on an oxygen machine. With hardly any teeth in her mouth and confined to a motorized wheelchair.

I loved and miss my big sister Doll very much; she was a true "Queen Madam" if you ask me. My brother-in-law (her husband), Leo was fine, fine, fine. Do you hear me?? When I say fine, picture Prince, because that is how fine and smooth my brother-in-law was.

He dressed extremely well. Before I even knew what "eye candy" was, women was considering him "eye candy" for sure.

He was mulatto, with beautiful eyes, good hair and all the features of a movie star. OMG! this man was just fine, fine, fine.

From what I understand, his family was from Connecticut. I was told all kinds of interesting stories about him and my sister "back in the day".

Once I was told that back in the day, Leo was once a Pimp from Connecticut and my sister was his Queen Madam. I am not sure how true all of that was because as I said, they were much older than me. Although I do remember that they were married and could dress their behinds off. OMG, the way they danced. Their specialty was hand dancing and they could hand dance like crazy.

These two should have been in movies the way they danced. They looked like professionals. They were on point! Dot your I's cross your T's excellent dancers. Slow, fast, it didn't matter.

Whenever Doll and Leo would come around (when I was younger), everyone would be hoping they would start dancing. The show "Dancing with the Stars" had nothing on them.

Leo would spin Doll around, and around and around and then let go of her hand and she would never miss a beat dancing with him, coming out those multiple spins.

I remember once, they were dancing at one of our mother's birthday parties. This time, it was the fast hand dance, not the slow one. The song; New Birth "I can understand it" was playing and I can still hear and remember that day so clearly;

Lyrics:

> "Jack and Jill going up the hill,
> storybook and fairy tales
> I, I can understand it"

They look so beautiful dancing. They were just a beautiful couple. Two Confident strong beautiful individuals.

Dark skin Baby Doll and fine as wine Leo.

Their true partnership showed every time. I later found out that my sister had no choice but to be perfect in what she did with him because as I said, he had a "pimp daddy" style. Therefore, if she wasn't on point, I was told she got hit.

My sister was talking to someone (I can't recall who it was), however, she was screaming at the top of her lungs that my brother-in-law strip her close off of her and beat her with a belt and sometimes the buckle. This was to avoid hitting her in open areas people could see.

She was indeed well trained by him but what else could one expect. The two of them were childhood sweethearts, so they grew up into adult hood together.

I remember one day Doll took me with her uptown to my brother-in-law's sister's house. His sister's name was (let's just call her Lisa), and Lisa was so beautiful.

This entire family was simply gorgeous, every last one of them, the girls and the boys. Just amazingly beautiful looking people.

I was such a young girl and I loved to make up my own songs and sing them to Doll. I was scared as heck to sing to people but not Doll. She was different.

She made me feel comfortable when I sang to her. Heck, she would sing with me. She even added stuff when she was helping me make up songs. She was a lot of fun.

Doll was extremely close with her sister in-laws. One day she asked our mother if I could go with her to visit her sister in-law Lisa.

Mother loved Leo and his family, so she said "yes, of course, and tell Lisa I said hi".

I can't quite remember where it was, but what I do remember is it was a long ride. It took about 1 hour or more to get there, from our neighborhood and it was beautiful! It look totally different from where we lived and too me Kentland was also beautiful but nothing like this. This was TV Hollywood beautiful.

This place had huge mansion homes, a lake, security entrance and more. I remember thinking to myself, wow, this must be where the rich and beautiful people live.

Lisa was so beautiful and always very nice. When we arrived, she and my sister started chatting, and then they went into one of Lisa back bedrooms.

When they came out, I don't know what it was, but she said "oh, lets us not forget this" and gave my sister something in a bag.

They chatted for a little longer, and Lisa played with me a little, tickling me and asked me questions about how I liked school and what I wanted to be when I grew up.

My sister Doll said, "she wants to be a songwriter and singer, and she's going to be just that because she's already good at it".

As she looked at me, gave me a head nod, smile and winked her eye. She told Lisa that, I could sing really well but was very shy and how Diana Ross was my favorite singer.

She also told her how I would often put a towel on my hair and swing it, with a brush in my hand pretending I was Diana Ross.

Lisa said to me "little Peaches (my nickname) you like to sing?" I smiled blushing, saying nothing.

She then said, "hold on. Let me let you talk to someone, a friend of mine". She picked up the phone and called a man, said something and then gave me the phone.

She said, "here… say hello to one of the most famous singers you will ever get the chance to talk to" (Name has been omitted to protect their privacy). I was so young, I said, "for real?? It's really him?" She and my sister started laughing and said, "yes ma'am. Talk to him".

I didn't know what to say. I don't even know if it was really him, but to me, it was him on Lisa's phone, at least I believed it was at that time. It sounded just like him to me. I will never forget that day. As I said, I was a young kid, and to this day, I don't know if it was really him, but I still feel good about that moment. I was so hyped up that my sister Doll stopped at the record store on our way home and bought me the Album "Songs in the Key of Life". I still have that Album to this day.

As I grew up and became a parent myself, I remember speaking to other celebrities on the phone. However, no one made an impact on me as that call did, when I was just a little girl.

I remember a radio station invited listeners to call in to get some advice from a guess speaker they had in the stations. I decided to call into the radio station now, most of the time, whenever I tried to call, the call would never get through, but this time, it did. This time, I know it was the real deal.

At that time, I was recently divorced after being married for 16 years. We were together for a total of 26 years. I had started dating again, which was very scary to me since my first husband was my high school sweetheart.

I shared with her information about this man that I had recently started dating. She listened to me and spoke one word, "Commitment". She said to me "it sounds like this man you are dating wants you to be fully committed to him, but he doesn't want to be fully committed to you". I will never forget what she said to me because it was so true. A woman who was and is still well known for her knowledge. That was another best experience of my life. The great Poet Ms. Maya Angelou.

You can feel the power of certainty in the words she spoke. Even now, when I read or hear her words, it brings joy. To know that I had the chance to speak with the gifted poet, always fills my heart with Joy. Just her name alone (to me) is beautiful. She was a remarkable woman.

One day my other Brother in-law CB (best brother-in-law anyone could ever have), told us a "back in the day" story about when he and Leo were young adults.

CB said that one day he and Leo were hanging out and they met a famous singer who was also very well known by his dancing.

After, I heard the story I believe, it turns out, I could have really been speaking to that famous person on Lisa's phone after all because apparently Leo and his sister Lisa were well known, and they knew famous people very well.

Here is what I can recall.

I remember that CB said Leo knew the famous James Brown. Not only did he know him, but he knew him really well.

CB said that Leo knew that famous singer so well that one time the two of them (CB and Leo) were hanging out and they saw a long line where people were standing outside a concert hall waiting to go in to see Mr. Brown himself perform.

They were just riding by and CB said to Leo "man that cat is a bad dude. Look at all those people standing in line waiting to see him".

Leo "CB, you like him? You want to go meet him?" CB started laughing, "man get the heck (but the F word) out of here!

You know damn well you don't know him!" He actual thought he was joking.

Leo, "Nah man, serious. You want to meet the cat? He's a cool brother".

CB said the next thing he knew, they were backstage in the dressing room with the one and only Mr. James Brown himself. James was giving Leo hugs and daps and all kinds of love.

CB couldn't believe it. Leo actually knew this cat, and knew him well, well enough to where James was calling Leo by his last name Fowler.

They got to see some of the show, free of charge and they didn't even have to stand in line.

They stayed and saw part of the show, then they rolled out due to other engagements Leo had to attend to.

Most likely, not sure but possibly money-making deals. What I can remember is that he also worked as a roofer at least that is what I was told.

The other thing I remember about Leo was that he stayed in and out of jail a lot. However, when he was home, he was well respected.

Also once heard a conversation that Leo like to flying high in the friendly sky from time to time. I thought that met, fly on an airplane. I later found out differently.

I remember one day when Leo came to our house to visit, my big brother snuck into his leather black jacket pocket.

My big brother was a sneaky cat. He would always do something that would get on a lot of people nerves. We love him very much, but he just sometimes do crazy things.

Here is what I recall;

We were all upstairs playing and listing to music and my big brother decided to sneak into Leo's coat pocket while no one was around and pulled out this black case.

I guess in his mind he was going to give us what he thought was perhaps a lesson on don't do drugs. He was a little jealous that everyone of us including mom loved Leo so much. Perhaps because he was so nice and so darn good to look at. Anyway, my big brother called us downstairs and said, "look what I found in Leo's coat pocket". Now my little brother and I didn't have a clue on what it was, but It was a needle and some type of black-tie thingy.

At the time, I had no idea what it was, I was extremely young, and my baby brother was even younger than I was. Therefore, he felt the need to teach us and started explaining to us what it was and how it works. He said, "see Peaches, this is drugs and he do drugs."

Right after he said that, my other two older siblings (brother and sister) came running down the stairs screamed at him "put it back and leave his stuff alone!". They looked at me and my little brother and said "go back upstairs and play.

My brother did his little sneaky laugh and put it back in Leo's coat pocket. My little brother and I ran back upstairs, while, my big brother went out the front door, which was near the steps.

Nevertheless, Leo always treated me kind and the fact I was just a young kid at that time, who really didn't know much about drugs, it never made a difference to me.

That's all I'll say about that. Unfortunately, Leo died from pneumonia.

Chapter 14

BUDGET TO TIGHT

My big brother, although I love him dearly, was good for trying to make you see what he felt was the truth about someone else.

I never paid him much attention because his character, as I saw it growing up, was pretty much, as they say, "off the chain".

I mean, one minute he was sweet and then the next minute, he would flip the script, and all of a sudden. He was straight up weird.

He did stuff I thought was truly crazy. Stuff like dropping out of school in 12th grade because (and these are his words to my mother), "a white boy who sits next to me is smarter than me. So how they going to graduate both of us?"

Yes, to him, he wasn't going to let "the man" let him graduate dummier than the white boy who set next to him. By the time my mother knew anything about it, it was way too late.

He had already dropped out and she didn't even know it. The school had informed her that there was nothing he could do except repeat the 12th grade, which he certainly wasn't going to do.

I remember one time when we were young, my big brother was in the living room watching TV and some of us went in to watch it with him because we only had one TV back then. Apparently, he was high from smoking marijuana.

I remember the TV being turned down so low that you could see the lips moving but you couldn't hear anything....not one single word.

He was sitting on the floor with his hands folded behind his head looking at the TV, eyes blood shot red, high as a kite....just smiling.

We were all screaming "turn the TV up boy!!" And this dude said in a whispering voice, "if you just be really quite and listen, you will be able to hear it. You just have to listen".

I am not sure if it was my mother or one of my other older siblings who may have been over, (my two oldest sisters, didn't live in the Kentland house), but somebody finally came in the living room and went over and turned the TV volume up for us.

I do remember he started laughing like crazy as he got up off the floor to leave the room.

Although he did a lot of crazy and weird things while I was growing up, he also did a lot of good things as well.

I heard he also once saved a boy's life when he was out whitewater rafting.

He's weird at times, truly nuttier than a fruit cake, but he also has some good qualities about him as well. Very nice personality indeed, always showed his respect to families who may have lost a love one. Always go visiting during the Christmas holidays to the elders and take them a Pie or flowers. He truly is a nice guy at times.

However, just to name a few weird things he did…

once when he was married and lived in a beautiful home with his wife and children. My sister-in-law (his wife), shared with me that he told her and their children, that their family was on a tight budget. Therefore, there would be only a certain amount of rolls of toilet tissue that they could use per week. If they ran out, no matter if they still have toilet paper put up for the next week, they would have to use a piece of paper bag until it's "Toilet Paper" time again, because they on a budget.

My sister-in-law said she told him nope, that is not happening in this house, and that was it, she put her foot down and that did not happen in their house. As she told us the story, she had us all laughing. She said she asked him if he had lost his mind.

Of course, he didn't get his way because my sister-in-law was time enough for him. I guess that's why she could put up with his crazy antics and they've been married for such a long time.

As I said, I love my family all of them and it was five of us who lived in the Kentland house. This series 1, I hope you got an understanding of how wonderful my mother love was. Stay tune for **Kentland Cooper's Series II (Bloodline Illness)** as I share more memories about my family, friends and career.

The Author of this book dedicates this book to the memories of her loving mother. Thank you for being the best mom ever!

She also gives credit and thank you to all her family members and friends.

Thank you all for your support and encouragement over the years.

To my children, thank you for being awesome terrific kids.

Deana M, Frances D. Shena D. I can always count on you to tell me what I "need" to hear, and not always what I "want" to hear. Thank you for being true friends.

To my Christian sister, Carla R. Thank you for your kind words and spiritual guidance. You help encourage me to hold on to his unchanging hand through the second hardest times in my life. Your support and spiritual guidance helped me make it through.

To Mr. Kevin M. and Mr. Ralph L. Although you may not even be aware. God allowing you to enter into my life at the time you did was not an accident. Thank you for being who you are. May you continue to be blessed always.

To my husband, children, sisters, brothers, nieces, nephews and all. Thank you for believing in me, I love you guys so much. This book is our family legacy.

To my late mom, dad, sister and brother. You may be gone, but you will never be forgotten. I love you and miss you dearly.

Love Always

Peaches
AKA Aya Emanuel